Encouragement for America's Hidden Heroes

Survival Tactics for the Families of Our Military Forces

By

Amy Stevens

authorHOUSE

1663 LIBERTY DRIVE, SUITE 200
BLOOMINGTON, INDIANA 47403
(800) 839-8640
www.authorhouse.com

© 2004 Amy Stevens
All Rights Reserved.

No part of this book may be reproduced, stored in a retrieval system, or transmitted by any means without the written permission of the author.

First published by AuthorHouse 07/26/04

ISBN: 1-4184-7047-3 (sc)
ISBN: 1-4184-7048-1 (dj)

Library of Congress Control Number: 2004094010

Printed in the United States of America
Bloomington, Indiana

This book is printed on acid-free paper.

Table of Contents

Introduction ix

Pre-deployment Survival Tactics 1
    1. Stay positive 2
    2. Analyze Your Current Situation 3
    3. Update your ID card 5
    4. Set up support networks 6
    5. Analyze your expected pay 7
    6. Set up an outsourcing plan 8
    7. Set up a budget 10
    8. Understand your family finances 11
    9. Familiarize yourself with the Military pay system 12
    10. Take advantage of Active benefits 13
    11. Become familiar with your insurance plan 15
    12. Select and interview doctors 17
    13. Update life insurance policies 18
    14. Obtain a Power of Attorney 19
    15. Create a will for yourself 20
    16. Create a file for all military-related documents 21
    17. Ignore gossip about orders! 22

Survival during a deployment 23
    Emotional Needs: 24
    18. Stay positive 24
    19. Pray 25
    20. Cry 26
    21. Laugh 27
    22. Lighten up on yourself 28
    23. Schedule a time for de-stressing 29
    24. Exercise for your health 30
    25. Encourage your spouse 31

    Actions to Take: 32
    26. Ask for help 32
    27. Have lists of "needs" 33
    28. Carry yourself proudly 34
    29. Avoid isolating yourself 35

30. Avoid being a victim 36
31. Give attention to what <u>you</u> feel is important 37
32. Expect the unexpected 38
33. Exercise Patience 39
34. Watch the news sparingly 40
35. Volunteer 41
36. Get involved 42
37. Learn 43
38. Educate others 44
39. Talk about and develop other interests 45
40. Make improvement plans 46
41. Measure your progress 48
42. Keep a journal 49
43. Establish email networks 50
44. Take care of business! 51
45. Celebrate your successes! 52
46. Don't listen to gossip about orders! 53

Family 55
47. Stay positive 56
48. Tell your children the truth 57
49. Educate your children 58
50. Send letters and packages frequently 59
51. Record the children's events 60
52. Take family outings 61
53. Set up time with other military families 62
54. Understand your children's emotions 63
55. Keep discipline consistent 64
56. Work on projects together 65
57. Establish a routine 66
58. Shake up the routine 67
59. Make the most of long-distance communication 68
60. Keep kids away from CNN 69
61. Explain others' behaviors 70
62. Count your blessings together 71

Your relationship 73
63. Stay positive 74
64. You are serving your country, too! 75
65. Make the most of long-distance communication 76
66. Eliminate guilt from your spouse 77

Homecoming 79
    67. Stay positive 80
    68. Research and prepare emotionally 81
    69. Research and understand medications 82
    70. Have realistic expectations for readjustment 83
    71. Exercise patience with your spouse 84
    72. Celebrate! 85
    Resources for the Military family: 87

Introduction

This book was written to honor, guide, and connect with the military families who are currently serving their country: by supporting their service member. While my husband was serving in Afghanistan, it became apparent to me that there are many families and spouses who have had no preparation or guidance, and for whom the military experience is quite new. There are many books on how to navigate the military bases, proper etiquette, rank issues, and how to move your family every few years, but I was unable to find a book with practical advice for a combat deployment separation. Many of us are facing War for the first time in our lives, and we have not been sufficiently trained or prepared emotionally for this experience.

I understand the fears, worries, stressors and pressures that burden a military family. As the wife of an Infantry officer, I dealt with a wide variety of emotions while running my own business and caring for our two sons. My experience allowed me to develop tactics and techniques that I would like to share with the other military spouses, who may be faced with a deployment in the near future.

As Reservists and National Guardsmen are called upon to join our Active military forces, I felt it even more appropriate to publish guidelines, suggestions, ideas, "must-do's", "should-do's", and "wish I'd dones" for those spouses who are entering into this phase of their lives, so that they may be prepared, and so that the may know that they, too, will survive. At the time of this publication, our country has 176,000 Reservists and National Guardsmen currently on Active Duty, either at home or abroad. The success of our Military forces can be enhanced by the capable, prepared families that can operate successfully while they are away.

Throughout this book I use the word spouse whenever possible, as opposed to writing specifically from the perspective of a "wife". Husbands, fathers, wives, and mothers are all deployed to various locations in support of our country. This book will give each group useful tactics and a variety of issues to consider and ponder.

I would like to thank my wonderful family: Mom, Dad, Leah and kids, Jackie, Perry, Jim, Sally and kids, Patti and kids, Tom, Monette, Becky and Donnie and kids; each of you made such a difference for us during this deployment. Craig and Lisa, thank you to you for your support and understanding. Randy and Peri: thank you for the wonderful pictures (on back cover). To the military wives on email: I appreciate you! To Cal, Max, and the other SOD soldiers who contacted me: thank you! I'd also like to acknowledge my supportive and loving church family, Northwest Fellowship, and my many friends and business associates that helped me through this time.

Most importantly, however, I want to acknowledge my husband Brian, who I am truly proud of; and my wonderful boys, JP and Hunter; the little soldiers who served their country beautifully.

To the reader: I hope that my experience may make your path easier….. May God Bless our Troops and their Families……

Encouragement for America's Hidden Heroes

Pre-deployment
Survival Tactics

1. Stay positive

I begin each section with the words "Stay Positive". Although it is easier said than done, it will be your key to survival during a military combat deployment. Start practicing now! Take each day that your family has together and enjoy it.

There is often a period prior to a deployment, where both parties begin to "separate" emotionally. The soldier is beginning to get his "game face" on, to best prepare for the challenges ahead. The family is beginning to get anxious and fearful; both regarding their upcoming responsibilities and sacrifices and over concern for the safety of their loved one. This is a time when there can be some uncharacteristic emotional moments, arguments, or fights. By preparing for this, and committing to be as positive as possible, you will ensure that your time together will be less frustrating and more enjoyable.

Support your soldier, work together on plans, and make time for each other. This time will always be special, and you can make quality memories that will last through the deployment.

The soldiers that I've spoken with assure me that leaving a spouse who is confident about the separation, supportive of the mission, and emotionally ready for the challenges ahead, allows them to fully commit to their job and to perform as needed during their deployment.

Believe in yourself…you can do it!

The happiness of your life depends on the qualities of your thoughts.— Marcus Aurelius

---

Questions to consider:

1) What do I enjoy doing with my spouse?

2) What can we do together before the deployment?

3) How can we best remain positive during this time?

2. Analyze Your Current Situation

Take some time to address your current work schedule, your child care arrangements (if any) and other aspects of your life that may change once you are alone. The pre-deployment phase is a good time to analyze what may need to change for you in order to optimize your priorities.

I created the following 4-step process for making decisions under stressful situations:

    A. What are your priorities?
    B. What is the ideal state of events needed to fully support your priorities?
    C. What is the current state of events?
    D. What actions can help you move from the current state to the ideal state?

I discovered that every small step that I took to move me from my current state to my ideal state gave me a feeling of success, and allowed me to exercise some control over the situation. Decisions became much easier, and I was able to align my life, commitments, and actions with my priorities for our family. Through this process, I decided to leave a job, start my business, and take other actions that gave me more time with my children.

It's a very simple tool to remember and use, and will help provide a step by step map for reaching the state of events that are important for your priorities.

Look well into thyself; there is a source which will always spring up if thou wilt always search there.—Marcus Aurelius

---

Questions to consider:

1) What are my priorities?

2) Review B, C, and D above for each priority that you determine is important.

3) How will I begin on my actions?

4) When will I begin taking these actions?

Encouragement for America's Hidden Heroes

3. Update your ID card

Ensure that your spouse accompanies you to the nearest location where you can update your ID card, if it is danger of expiring during the deployment. This card will allow you to get onto military bases, shop at the PX, and take advantage of many military discounts across the country.

We found many discounts for military families, including Sea World, various restaurants, zoos and entertainment facilities. I also used my ID to get on different military posts to shop, to visit injured soldiers, or to take care of pending business for my husband.

Without the ID card, it is very difficult to get past security on military bases or hospitals. I want to ensure that our Security officers are not busy with the military families, but doing the important job of protecting the bases for all of us.

Once a decision was made, I did not worry about it afterward. –Harry S. Truman

---

Questions to consider:

1) Where can I take advantage of military discounts?

2) Is there a PX where I can shop or services that my family can take advantage of?

4. Set up support networks

Pre-deployment is the time to think about who you have to depend on, and who can be called upon in case of emergency or need.

I have been blessed to have family in the area, a wonderful church whose members truly reached out to my family, and long-time friends and neighbors. Many ladies I encountered did not have this arrangement initially, but chose to use the pre-deployment time to get to know other ladies in the same situation, and to reach out to their neighbors.

If you are unsure where to find support, I would recommend visiting a church, getting involved in your children's schools or sports teams, or connecting with other families whose soldiers are deploying with your spouse. If you have been contacted by or assigned to a Family Readiness Unit, please get involved and find out who will be in the same situation soon, where they live, and how to contact them. If you have not yet been contacted by a Family Readiness Unit, make sure that your spouse gets you in touch with the appropriate person, and that you are listed correctly so that others may find you as well.

You may not need any help while your spouse is away, but knowing where it lies can relieve some of your burden.

What God expects us to attempt, He also enables us to achieve. –Stephen Olford

---

Questions to consider:

Who can I reach out to for help?

How could these people help me?

What actions will I take to find support?

5. Analyze your expected pay

Along the lines of the previous survival tactic, I am again stressing the need to analyze your expected pay. For many Reservists who may have their own businesses, may work for small companies, or may have other income fluctuations, they may find that the military pay is quite short of what they have become accustomed to.

According to Meredith Leyva, in "Married to the Military", thousands of Reservists lost all their savings when they were called to duty in Operation Iraqi Freedom. Why? Their Military pay was much less than their civilian pay, and they were forced to make up the difference from their own savings. (Leyva, 71).

I personally know of several men who served with my husband in Afghanistan, who faced this issue. Financial stress on top of the emotional upheavals associated with having a loved one in harm's way can be extremely difficult for the spouse at home.

Take the pre-deployment time to determine what your situation will be, so that you will not be surprised once you are alone. Research the financial assistance and relief that can be provided by the Soldiers and Sailors Federal Relief Act (Tip # 10) By doing this, you give yourself the time to adjust, plan, and budget so that you can emerge from this deployment financially successful!

We are restless because of incessant change, but we would be frightened if change were stopped. –Lyman Lloyd Bryson

---

Questions to consider:

What will my spouse's paycheck look like each month?

What amount is he/she currently making each month?

How will I use the extra money…. or where will I cut expenses if the paycheck is smaller?

6. Set up an outsourcing plan

Since my husband was an Active Duty National Guardsman, we found that he received additional pay as a result of his deployment to Afghanistan. We received a Family Separation Allowance, Hostile Fire Pay (which doesn't cover my opinion of what he's worth!), and had the income tax relief afforded to those in combat zones.

Because we researched the expected pay ahead of time, I was able to see clearly that we could pay for someone to deep clean my home once per month, and for an independent landscaper to mow my lawn. These simple "outsourcing" measures saved me many hours of stress!

We identified where I would take the cars, who I would call for the air conditioner and other appliances, and which of his friends had volunteered to help me. I had phone numbers, email addresses, brochures and websites all at my fingertips for any needs that might come about. This gave me a sense of confidence in areas that I had not previously involved in, and made the tasks more manageable when issues did arise.

By researching and planning, we were able to effectively prepare for our separation, and to anticipate upcoming stressors.

Trouble creates a capacity to handle it. –Oliver Wendell Holmes, Jr.

Questions to consider:

What potential needs might I have during this time?

Who will I contact?

Who are our service providers?

    Car
    Home

Exterminators
Plumbers
Others

7. Set up a budget

This tactic is for all families of our military. Whether you choose to get advice from a certified financial planner, the military sources, or the internet, it is imperative that you have a plan.

I found that the "extra" money seemed to disappear rather quickly, whereas my intention was to save money during this time. I learned that establishing a budget allowed us to make better progress, reach goals, and survive day to day in a much happier way.

A wonderful resource for budgeting advice is the section "Creating a Balanced Budget", from the book "Heroes at Home" by Ellie Kay. She gives many tips for saving money, includes case studies, and provides a template for your use. There is also a website, www.savvy.onweb.com, where you may purchase the book "The Savvy Sailor", a book detailing military financial planning. It is written from the perspective of a sailor, but all service members can benefit from its advice.

Moderation is the key to lasting enjoyment.—Hosea Ballou

Questions to consider:

1) How much money do I need to pay our family's monthly expenses?

2) Where can I save on our current expenses?

8. Understand your family finances

There are still many families today where one person is totally in control of all financial decisions, bill paying, and asset management. The pre-deployment time is the best opportunity for you to begin taking over this activity, if you are not already the primary financial person in your family.

Knowing where accounts are, what needs to be paid, where the money is, and *how much* money there is are critical elements to running a smooth home while your spouse is away. You should also know where important documents and account numbers are located, and ensure that you have adequate access privileges.

Take the time together to explore this area of responsibility, so that it does not become a burden. Set up a plan or use a software solution such as *Quicken* to make this task easier and less time consuming.

Arriving at one goal is the starting point to another.—John Dewey

---

Questions to consider:

1) What bills need to be paid, and when?

2) What bank accounts, CD's, or investments do we have?

3) Where are the account numbers and associated documents?

9. Familiarize yourself with the Military pay system

A very helpful tool for the spouse at home is the "My Pay" website: www.dfas.mil. This site allows you to view your spouse's LES (past, present, and upcoming), and provides other financial links and information.

Ensure that you log on to the site together, create a password, and become familiar with how to use it. It was a resource for me in understanding the pay fluctuations that occur with a deployed spouse, and helped me plan our finances much more effectively than waiting for the LES to arrive.

A wonderful resource for the new military family is the website: www.cinchouse.com. As in her book, "Married to the Military", Meredith Leyva details information on many topics, from how to read an LES to what to do if your pay is incorrect.

To know just what has to be done, then to do it, comprises the whole philosophy of practical life.—Sir William Osler

---

Questions to consider:

1) "My Pay" user name and password

2) Notes: Things to look for on my spouse's paycheck (hostile fire pay, family separation allowance, etc.)

10. Take advantage of Active benefits

Particularly for National Guardsmen and Reservists, there are several advantages to having a spouse who is deployed on Active Duty. One of these is the Soldiers and Sailors Relief Act, which provides support for those called to serve.

If you're a reserve component service member called to active duty, you're protected by a law that can save you some legal problems and possibly some money as well. Under the provisions of the Soldiers' and Sailors' Civil Relief Act of 1940, you may qualify for any or all of the following:

> Reduced interest rate on mortgage payments.
> Reduced interest rate on credit card debt.
> Protection from eviction if your rent is $1,200 or less.
> Delay of all civil court actions, such as bankruptcy, foreclosure or divorce proceedings.

We used this Act to reduce our home mortgage interest rate from 7% to 6% during Brian's deployment, which was a nice corresponding reduction in our monthly payment.

By contacting your mortgage company or others who you have credit from, you can discuss with them their procedures for enacting this benefit.

The world hates change, yet it is the only thing that has brought progress.—Charles F. Kettering

---

Questions to consider:

1) What debts do we currently owe with interest rates above 6%?

2) What creditors do I need to contact?

3) How much money will be saved per this Act, and how will I invest or spend it?

4) Do I have serious concerns currently about eviction or bankruptcy?

11. Become familiar with your insurance plan

This tactic may not be relevant for families who are living on a military base, as the medical care and procedures will not change for you. However, for many Reservists and their families, the military insurance, rules, and procedures may be difficult to navigate at first. Take the time to learn about your health plan, collect your documents, and talk with a TRICARE representative first-hand. I found them to be extremely helpful, happy to answer my questions, and pleasant to speak with.

Your spouse's unit may have an information session specifically for the families. If so, I urge you to attend and participate so that you understand your benefits and the requirements. Talk with other families who have been covered under TRICARE, so that you can gain knowledge from some of their experiences.

If you have specific medical needs that require Specialists, or where there is a sensitive issue regarding yourself or your children where a particular doctor is necessary, please do not be afraid to discuss this with TRICARE and with contacts at your Family Readiness Unit. Though many Civilian doctors do not accept TRICARE, I have seen situations where exceptions have been made in extreme circumstances.

You may find the TRICARE website at the following address: www.tricare.osd.mil.

For Dental coverage, families of Active service members may acquire inexpensive dental insurance through United Concordia, www.ucci.com, which will allow your family access to a large network of civilian providers.

Readjusting is a painful process, but most of us need it at one time or another. –Arthur Christopher Benson

Questions to consider:

1) Which insurance plan covers my family?

2) Did the website answer my questions and explain what I need?

3) Do I need to speak with someone to clarify any details?

12. Select and interview doctors

There are few things more frustrating, upsetting, and exhausting to a parent than having a sick child. Trying to figure out where to go, how to get an appointment, or who to go to compounds the misery of all involved.

Take the time before your spouse deploys to select your doctor, understand their hours and emergency procedures, and ensure that you know how to handle a medical situation. Reservists and National Guardsmen may be able to use military facilities, or may need to select new doctors who accept TRICARE. You may search for physicians on the TRICARE website: www.tricare.osd.mil.

If you do not recognize the doctors listed on the website, use this occasion to contact the families of other soldiers who may have gone through the selection process already, and who may have a wealth of advice for you. We have a wonderful family physician, for example, who is less than 2 miles from our home and who gladly accepts TRICARE. I have shared this resource on many occasions.

By handling these issues prior to your spouse's deployment, you will help ensure that you feel confident and calm in case urgent situations arise.

We either make ourselves miserable, or we make ourselves strong. The amount of work is the same.—Carlos Castaneda

Questions to consider:

1) Do my current doctors accept TRICARE?

2) Which doctors will my family use?

3) Where are they located?

4) What are the hours and emergency numbers for the doctors I've selected?

13. Update life insurance policies

Many people choose not to talk about life insurance or the possibility that their spouse may be killed while on a military deployment. Although I certainly prefer not to think about this possibility, I believe that a prepared family will fare better than an unprepared family if the unthinkable were to happen. The military does provide some life insurance for the troops, but I was not comfortable that it was enough for our needs as a family.

Analyze the amount of the insurance you are currently provided by the military, and determine what costs you would be immediately faced with (paying off a home? Other debts?) It is also wise to think about the yearly salary of your spouse, and how many years the life insurance will support your family.

I chose to supplement our insurance, and did find two companies that would insure a person in combat: USAA and AAFMAA. Contact them for rates for your spouse and yourself. www.usaa.com; and www.aafmaa.com. There are many other companies as well, but I felt that these two companies understood my situation and supported our troops, so I chose to go to them first. USAA also provides very competitive rates for service members on insurance; for both auto and home.

Security can only be achieved through constant change, through discarding old ideas that have outlived their usefulness and adapting others to current facts. –William O. Douglas

Questions to consider:

1) Do I have (or need) life insurance for my spouse?

2) Do I have (or need) life insurance for myself?

3) Insurance quotes and notes:

14. Obtain a Power of Attorney

During the pre-deployment phase, your spouse will be given an opportunity to meet with the Military legal entities regarding creation of a Power of Attorney. This document allows you to sign for your spouse on either general, or very specific situations, such as applying for credit, purchasing or selling a home, or refinancing debts.

My experience indicates that some establishments are somewhat leery of this "power" associated with the power of attorney. I was frequently asked for copies of my husband's orders, was usually transferred to "management" and had a somewhat difficult time actually using the document.

I believe it was certainly better than NOT having any "power" on his behalf, however, and the *full power of attorney* was more useful than one created for a specific situation. I urge you to take the initiative to get this document in order before your spouse deploys.

We must therefore take account of this changeable nature of things and of human institutions, and prepare for them with enlightened foresight.
–Pope Pius XI

Questions to consider:

1) Is there a specific situation where I need a power of attorney? (selling or buying a home, for example)

2) Will I act responsibly and with integrity while signing on my spouse's behalf?

15. Create a will for yourself

While your spouse is updating his or her will along with the pre-deployment paperwork, it is a good time for you to also create or update a will for yourself.

There are a number of attorneys who will charge a minimal rate for a basic will to be drawn up. I chose to get a membership to Pre-Paid Legal Services, for about $17.00 per month. Through their service, I was eligible to have a will created, and have a specified number of hours available to me to consult with attorneys as needed. Their site is www.prepaidlegal.com.

The will allowed me to clearly specify what will happen to my children if I were to be killed, and if my husband was out of the country and unable to be reached. I was concerned that there could potentially be a delay if this were to occur, and I wanted an explicit document stating who should care for my children until he could be reached.

It is important to send a copy of the will to the person who will have guardianship of the children, or who will be the executor of the will. In order for the will to be a helpful tool, someone must know that it exists.

Learn as if you're going to live forever. Live as if you're going to die tomorrow. –John Wooden

---

Questions to consider:

1) Do I have a will?

2) What arrangements would I like for a will to address?

16. Create a file for all military-related documents

By creating a file with your spouse's orders, your power of attorney, your TRICARE information and numbers, and any other important documents relating to the deployment, you become much more efficient and in control of your situation.

During my husband's deployment, I faxed the power of attorney and orders to quite a number of people while acquiring life insurance, attempting to refinance our home, and other types of business.

By having this information in one place, I was much better prepared when someone would ask for yet another copy of something. This reduced my time on the phone, the number of "call backs" which were required, and helped resolve situations quickly and efficiently. Though it seems like a small step, it is one that can save hours of time and frustration down the road.

> *None of us knows what the next change is going to be, what unexpected opportunity is just around the corner, waiting to change all the tenor of our lives.—Kathleen Norris*

Questions to consider:

1) What needs to be kept in this file?

2) Where will I keep the file?

17. Ignore gossip about orders!

During the pre-deployment phase, there was a constant "rumor mill" regarding when my husband would leave, how long the deployment would last, and many other so-called facts. We began worrying in February, and he didn't actually depart the state until June. In February we thought he was heading to Iraq, but in June he left for Afghanistan.

Well-meaning friends and relatives often keep you talking about your spouse's departure constantly, and keep you on edge. A good response is "It's the Army. It changes its mind…so we'll let you know when we know for certain".

Other wives and families may also be calling to share what they "heard" from someone else. I urge you to try to relax and minimize the gossip. Hold your emotions in check until the word is official. Enjoy your time together.

One must never lose time in vainly regretting the past or in complaining against the changes which cause us discomfort, for change is the essence of life. –Anatole France

---

Questions to consider:

1) How can I best respond to the questions that people ask my family?

2) How can I best respond to the gossip?

Survival during a deployment

Emotional Needs:

18. Stay positive

I again begin this section with the words "Stay Positive". In the pre-deployment phase, you were advised to stay positive in order to enjoy the time you had left with your spouse. In this phase, you are advised to stay positive in order to be fully functional yourself, to support your family and children, and to make the most out of this situation.

No amount of sadness or misery is going to change the orders for your spouse… so why put yourself through it? Why waste this part of your life? Seeking the joy in each situation will help you do more than survive; but thrive from day to day.

I know that there were certainly sad moments along the way, but I learned more, became stronger, and gained more confidence in this nine month period than in any other period of my life! By focusing on opportunity, I was able to see the blessings before me. Find those things that bring you happiness, and enjoy them often.

The happiest people seem to be those who have no particular cause for being happy except that they are so.—William Ralph Inge

---

Questions to consider:

1) What do I enjoy doing?

2) What really makes me happy?

3) How can I do these things often?

19. Pray

When people ask me how I managed to stay positive during my husband's deployment, I consistently say that I "prayed a lot".

Prayer was (and is) a way to release my burdens, to confide in our Heavenly father, and to ask for what I really needed. I prayed for protection for my husband and all of our troops, for comfort and understanding, for wisdom in dealing with the situation, and thanked God for my blessings.

In every case, I felt better, was brought closer to others who were praying for the troops, and became stronger in my faith. I was reminded that I am not in control of all things, which was relieving to me. I saw wonderful unions develop between those of us in prayer for our spouses, and saw the amazing results which were graciously given to us and to our families.

Unless I had the spirit of prayer, I could do nothing. –Charles G. Finney

Questions to consider:

1) What am I thankful for?

2) What do I need?

3) I will pray for _____.

There are two wonderful books that I enjoyed during this time, both published by Inspirio, The Gift Group of Zondervan, www.inspiriogifts.com:

1) Praying for Those We Love as They Serve Our Country

2) God Bless America: Prayers and Reflections for Our Country

20. Cry

There were days I encountered, where everything went wrong: I was convinced the kids were trying to make me crazy, I was overwhelmed with trying to run a business, my finances were out of control, I didn't feel well, and I was angry.

On these days, while trying to be "strong", I experienced physical manifestations of my stress in the form of headaches, stomach aches, and lightheadedness. I had numbness in my limbs on more than one occasion, neck pain, and back pain. I visited a trusted chiropractor to have her "adjust me", and what happened instead was a session of talking, crying, and admitting my fears.

Once I admitted these feelings to her and to myself, I realized that crying was a natural release of tension. I also learned that people were amazed that I hadn't cried more, or earlier, and that there were many people waiting in the wings to help me.

By learning that it was OK to cry, I was able to release the tension and start over in a positive way again. (At least for a few days or weeks!)

There are two days in the week about which and upon which I never worry… One of these days is yesterday… and the other day I do not worry about is tomorrow. –Robert Jones Burdette

---

Questions to consider:

1) What are my fears?

2) Is there someone I can talk to about these?

3) What makes my mood better?

21. Laugh

My wish for you is to fill your days with laughter, and to pay attention to those things that bring you true happiness. For me, the time with my children was hard to do alone, but the memories and laughter will be with me forever.

On one occasion, my 4 year old informed me that he "wanted a lawyer" when I was giving him time-out. My 2 year old screamed out "Silence" (or more like Si-wence) when my sister and I were having a heated discussion. Little moments come about that can make you *crack* or can make you *crack up!* It's all in the way you choose to view it.

When dealing with the children's emotions, I also found that creating a funny distraction proved much more valuable that trying to get into an emotional battle. They appreciated it, and we all benefited greatly.

The most thoroughly wasted of all days is that on which one has not laughed.—Nicolas de Chamfort

---

Questions to consider:

1) Funny things I want to remember:
    a. _____
    b. _____
    c. _____

2) Funny movies, websites, books, poems or uplifting quotes:
    a. _____
    b. _____
    c. _____

22. Lighten up on yourself

To my knowledge, there is no award for SuperSpouse, SuperMom (or Dad) or for the person who has the cleanest house, best dressed children, and everything perfectly arranged in their home and life.

I found that there are things that are more important to me: playing with my kids, actually eating dinner and talking with them, exercising, attending church, and relaxing. I wasted the first month alone with them trying to keep up all of the same standards that two people were doing before. This created stress for all of us, made me feel rushed and pressured, and was not adding value to our lives.

By lightening up on those things that are truly not important in the large scheme of life, we could more easily enjoy what things *were* important.

The way to develop self-confidence is to do the thing you fear and get a record of successful experiences behind you. –William Jennings Bryan

---

Questions to consider:

1) What can I "let go" for the time being?

2) What would I rather do with my time?

23. Schedule a time for de-stressing

I've always laughed at the articles and books that tell me to relax, go to a spa for a day, and to take care of myself. I thought "yeah, right". I'm a "single" mom right now, trying to run a business, with a million things to do, and I'm supposed to head to the spa?

In hindsight, I now think these people are less funny and probably right. I found that the spa was a bit of a stretch for me, but did decide to make time for myself to take a bath (gasp!), to read, or to pray. These things made a big difference for me, and I wish that I had implemented them sooner.

There should be no guilt associated with taking care of yourself. As my husband says, the wife at home is the "glue" holding everything together. Allowing for your own health and sanity helps everything else stay connected.

Write it on your heart that every day is the best day of the year. –Ralph Waldo Emerson

Questions to consider:

1) What will I do for myself each day, month, or week?

2) What helps me eliminate stress?

3) When can I take advantage of time alone?

24. Exercise for your health

I have always been an avid exerciser, and have always enjoyed it. When alone with two small children, however, the time seemed to slip away and there would be weeks when I wouldn't have time to exercise at all, or certainly not as much as I would have liked. We've all read about the health benefits of exercise, but I have never been as convinced of the mental benefits until this deployment. There was a dramatic difference in my overall outlook, ability to handle stress, and my feelings and confidence in myself during the periods when I faithfully exercised.

I found that there are many great videos on the market (though I prefer running our outdoor activity) that helped me during the days when I couldn't get away, or the weather wasn't good. I learned to enjoy yoga, Pilates, and other forms of exercise that I hadn't tried before.

I urge you to adapt to a program, set a time that works for you, and treat it as a priority. If you are healthy, you can better manage the deployment for you and your family.

A sound mind in a sound body is a short but full description of a happy state in this world. –John Locke

---

Questions to consider:

1) How can I best address my health?

2) What activities can I pursue?

25. Encourage your spouse

Most of our wonderful service men and women will go through periods of discontent, sadness, homesickness, fear, and worry while they are away. The greatest gift you can give your loved one is support, encouragement, and prayer.

Stand by your spouse, and put their emotional needs ahead of your own. This is a hard pill for some to swallow, but I stand firm in saying that anyone who is deployed, serving our country during wartime, and risking their life to protect mine DESERVES to have their emotional needs taken care of prior to those of us who are safely existing in our great country.

I am not suggesting that you fail to talk about how you feel, but please be aware that our lives, however stressful in their absence, is quite safe, calm and simple compared to our troops in combat. Pray for them, be strong for them, and take care of them. I believe that it is our duty as Americans to do so.

You cannot always have happiness, but you can always give happiness.
–Anon.

Questions to consider:

1) How can I encourage my spouse?

2) What will I communicate to my spouse?

Actions to Take:

26. Ask for help

During my husband's deployment, I was very fortunate to have a large network of people who were on "stand by" to help me and my family. Though I didn't ask for anything too significant, I did find that small calls to neighbors asking to borrow a thermometer (instead of carting a very sick 2 year old and a sleepy 4 year old to the store) helped me, and made them feel good as well. When I had really down days, I would invite someone over for dinner or call a friend. I asked for, and received, numerous prayers that helped me to feel less alone and much more comforted.

This behavior was unusual for me, as I always prided myself on being the "strong one" for my family and friends. Going through a combat deployment separation, however, demonstrated that being strong was not as important as being supported.

Don't forget to ask for help.

The healthy and strong individual is the one who asks for help when he needs it; Whether he's got an abscess on his knee, or in his soul. –Rona Barrett

---

Questions to consider:

1) Is there something that I need help with right now?

2) Important phone numbers:

27. Have lists of "needs"

If you foresee yourself having specific needs during your spouse's deployment, such as moving to a new home or having a baby, make sure that you plan ahead and list the things you'll need help with. Childcare arrangements, meals, or someone to take you to the hospital are all things that people truly want to help with!

Let someone know in your church, neighborhood, or family, what your needs are. It's a great idea to think about and have specific needs to share with people who ask to help. People can "sign up" for what works for them, and you'll have peace of mind. Your Family Readiness Unit may be a wonderful source of support during these situations as well.

Remember that we're all serving our country when we help a military family. Many people want to help…don't be afraid to ask.

Be brave enough to accept the help of others.—Melba Colgrove

Questions to consider:

1) What events do I need to plan for?

2) Who will I call?

3) What will I ask of them?

28. Carry yourself proudly

If only I could instill this feeling in all of the military spouses! I have seen many spouses who have worn their yellow ribbons, flag pins, spoken often about their husband and situation, and who represent the country well. I have also seen those who are playing the role of "victim", who are so sad, lonely, and miserable that they have lost sight of what it means to be a member of our military.

Though it may sound harsh, a military spouse has to understand that separations and potential combat deployments are always a real possibility. Of course I would rather have my husband at home, but serving our country is something that our family truly believes in and values. *I believe that we spouses are serving our great country by supporting our spouse and our President.* Many Americans look at us with pride, amazement, and wonder.

Carry yourself proudly and positively, to best represent all military families. This action will create a confidence in yourself, and remind you that your sacrifices are important.

Happiness comes from of the capacity to feel deeply, to enjoy simply, to think freely, to risk life, to be needed. – Storm Jameson

---

Questions to consider:

1) Am I proud of my spouse?

2) What specifically makes me feel proud of him/her?

3) How can I best communicate this to him/her?

4) How can I best remind myself of this?

29. Avoid isolating yourself

Isolation is a lonely, difficult road for the military spouse. I witnessed some spouses who did not want to get involved in anything new, and who even cut ties with groups and organizations that they were involved with before the deployment, because it was "too difficult" to go and answer questions and talk constantly about their situation.

Though I understand some elements of this sentiment, and even experienced difficulty getting too much sympathy from some friends, finding church hard to get through without my husband beside me, and other situations that caused some stress for me, they ultimately were much better for me and my children than sitting alone, isolating ourselves, watching the news, and getting depressed.

I was able to foster new, wonderful relationships that will now be mine for a lifetime, just by looking for them.

Happiness is not so much in having as sharing. We make a living by what we get, but we make a life by what we give. –Norman MacEwan

Questions to consider:

1) Is there anything that I am avoiding?

2) Would it make me feel better to resume this activity?

3) What would I like to do?

30. Avoid being a victim

I talked a bit about the "victim mentality" in an earlier tactic. I do not feel victimized in any way because my husband is called to duty to serve the USA. I chose to marry him, knowing that he was career military, and gladly and proudly stand by this choice.

Many of us live our entire lives without impacting the world in any profound way. I know that my job, though in the background, is one of the most critical and important jobs supporting the military. Supporting my husband does not seem to be a negative activity to me; it is an honor.

Remind yourself that you are serving your country, impacting another country, and teaching your children and family about patriotism. This is something to be proud of.

Self-pity is our worst enemy and if we yield to it, we can never do anything wise in this world. –Helen Keller

---

Questions to consider:

1) How can I feel pride in my situation?

2) What do I want to be "known for"?

3) What do I want my children to learn?

31. Give attention to what _you_ feel is important

In the daily existence of a working parent, there is rarely much time to ponder what is important to the parent, but merely a continued push to do what is important to others. Your children, other family members, neighbors, and well-meaning friends may try to distract you, keep you busy, or get you involved in what they believe is important or enjoyable.

If you agree, then enjoy yourself! If not, then politely let them know that you have plans, and honor that which you feel is important for your family and your time.

My family often had some of our best times together simply cooking dinner, eating, and reading together. No "entertainment" was necessary, and often this provided the best environment for true bonding and interaction.

If you do not find peace in yourself, you will never find it anywhere else.
—Paula A. Bendry

Questions to consider:

1) What am I doing because I "have to" for someone else?

2) Is there an activity I'm being pushed to do that causes me undue stress?

3) What do I want to do with my time?

32. Expect the unexpected

This tactic talks to both preparation and a mind-set. By preparing in the earlier tactics before deployment, some of the unexpected can be managed easily.

The mind-set I'm referring to is one of calmness and evenness. Things will happen, unusual events will occur, and you will have days where you think things are falling apart. By knowing this ahead of time, I hope that you can easily accept challenges, avoid excessive stress or surprise, and feel good in knowing that it happens to most of us!

I found that keeping extra time "cushions" in my schedule, and minimizing as much of our hectic routines as possible helped to allow time for the unexpected events.

Everything passes; everything wears out; everything breaks. – French proverb

Questions to consider:

1) When is my most "hectic" time of day?

2) When should I avoid scheduling more tasks?

3) When is the easiest time of day for me?

4) Do I want to protect this time of day, or schedule more activity here?

33. Exercise Patience

In this tactic, I am speaking of patience with your family, friends, situations, career, and yourself!

Most of us did not find that things moved as quickly as they did with our spouse present, and that simple actions before now take all day, week, or year with only one person attending to them. This is OK. Be patient, the deployment will go much faster than you think.

In the mean time, planning and organization can help move things along! Don't be afraid to make lists, write out goals, or modify your definition of success. I found that my business goals took a backseat to my parenting goals during our separation. By intentionally allowing myself to do this, I felt less like a failure in any area, and felt much more in control in every area.

The shortest answer is doing. –English proverb

Questions to consider:

1) What are my priorities? (review tactics 2 and 31)

2) Will creating lists help me?

34. Watch the news sparingly

I found that there seemed not to be very good time to watch the news. Mornings were hectic, the children were listening, and it didn't always help my day get off to the best start. Likewise, watching late at night didn't help me to sleep!

Since my husband was an Infantry officer serving in a combat zone, every news story, death, bombing, or other incident immediately received a visceral reaction from my body, and immediately changed my positive outlook to one of doom.

I found that I needed to know what was happening, but that I didn't need a play by play, minute by minute report. I finally determined that for me, the best way to stay informed was to watch a major news channel once per day, and to log in to the Afghan News Network every couple of days. I knew that I would be contacted if something specific to my husband were to occur, and I decided that I did not need to see every detail of the War.

This action alone helped me to have fewer stressful or tearful days.

It is our relation to circumstances that determines their influence over us. The same wind that carries one vessel into port may blow another offshore.—Christian Bovee

---

Questions to consider:

1) When will I watch the news (if at all)?

2) Websites where I can get information I need:

    a. www.foxnews.com
    b. www.afghannewsnetwork.net
    c. _____
    d. _____

35. Volunteer

One of the greatest opportunities before us as military spouses is to help others in our situation. This is why I've written this book, why I've spoken to groups on "life as a military wife", and why I organized letter campaigns for our troops, collected toys for an Afghan orphanage, and continually reached out to other families in need.

This involvement takes the burden off of you, forces you to look outside yourself, and allows you to grow. Through my experience, many other civilians were given the opportunity to "help", which was a blessing to them as well as the recipient of the help.

When we step outside of our own fears, worries and doubts to reach out to another, the focus changes to one of service...and the rewards feel wonderful.

The only ones among you who will be really happy are those who will have sought and found how to serve.—Albert Schweitzer

---

Questions to consider:

1) Who needs my help?

2) What services can I offer to others?

3) What would I enjoy providing to others?

36. Get involved

My church was an amazing place for support, comfort, encouragement, and peace. By getting involved, I was ministering to others, but also had the benefit of having people get to know me and my situation. Many people prayed for my family, sent us cards, and wrote my husband. This was truly comforting and humbling.

Likewise, my children's preschool treated our boys like celebrities, made posters and cards for the troops, and were very aware of what our boys were going through. Because of my involvement, more people became aware of our situation and could help our family. At the same time, I was able to meet treasured friends.

There were many people waiting to support me; all I had to do was share our situation with them and ask for their support.

There is nothing on this earth ore to be prized than true friendship. –Saint Thomas Aquinas

Questions to consider:

1) How could I get more involved with groups I'm currently attending?

2) What activities do I enjoy? How can I meet others in this area?

37. Learn

One of the most interesting things that happened during my husband's deployment was the transition I took from "military wife" to someone friends decided was an "expert on Afghanistan". I was obsessed with information initially to attempt to calm my fears, but after a while it became an interesting educational experience.

I learned about the various tribes in Afghanistan, read about their leaders, studied the history of the region, talked with my husband about the culture, and became truly informed about the true Afghanistan, and not just what is covered in our media.

This gave my husband and I an opportunity to talk about something that was of critical importance to him, and was a way for me to further support him and the other troops serving in that country.

The very first step towards success in any occupation is to become interested in it. –Sir William Osler

Questions to consider:

1) How can I learn more about the country my spouse is in?

2) Websites I found:

    a. _____
    b. _____
    c. _____

3) Books I'd like to read

    a. _____
    b. _____
    c. _____

38. Educate others

Through my studies and conversations with my husband, I found myself frequently involved in discussions about politics and our involvement in Afghanistan and Iraq. I was able to dispel some untruths first hand, and was sought out by friends and colleagues to answer questions and explain some areas to them in terms of the military perspective.

I was asked to speak on two occasions, to educate the audience, show some photographs of the Afghan people, and to help raise awareness of their needs. This was a truly rewarding experience, and I am continuing to enjoy the examination of the country and its people.

I was recently asked to join the Advisory Council of the Afghan Women's Project, an initiative founded by Peggy Kelsey in Austin, Texas. Through this involvement, I'm still able to reach out to the women of Afghanistan and to help raise funds for their health, wellness, and literacy. Peggy's site for the Afghan Women's Project is www.kelseys.net.

By reaching for knowledge, I expanded my own viewpoint and involvement in the world, and have been blessed by opportunities to share it with others.

Keep your fears to yourself, but share your courage with others. –Robert Louis Stevenson

---

Questions to consider:

1) How can I share what I've learned from this experience?

2) What would I like to share?

39. Talk about and develop other interests

Although it is definitely true that I spent a rather large amount of time answering questions and discussing my husband, I made a point not to talk about it unless asked. I also tried to demonstrate that there were many other things I enjoy talking about as well, including my children, family, marketing small businesses, running, the Bible, Religion, and funny stories.

One business associate let me know recently that she had no idea that my family was going through such a stressful time. This comment demonstrated to me that I had been successful in spending time on other interests, and that I had not allowed my grief to become an obsession.

Have a variety of interests… These interests relax the mind and lessen tension on the nervous system. People with many interests live, not only longest, but happiest.—George Matthew Allen

---

Questions to consider:

1) What are my interests?

2) Have I been neglecting my interests, or pursuing them?

3) What would I like to learn, do, or see?

40. Make improvement plans

When your spouse is away, it is easy to put yourself and your life into "wait" mode. I urge you to continue moving forward with your own plans for life, whether the plans focus on career, school, weight loss, exercise goals, piano lessons, or anything else that is important to you. Many ladies I talked with found great pleasure in redecorating, completing decks and other unfinished projects. Others (such as myself) start their own businesses. My company, Go Beyond Marketing, (www.gobeyondmarketing.com) is dedicated to helping other small businesses succeed in their marketing and planning. It's something I always wanted to do; so I did!

Regardless of the task or project you take on, we military wives agree that *waiting is harder than doing.*

Instead of counting down the days until you "get to" do something when your spouse comes home, you may find great reward in doing it anyway. My mother-in-law and I took 3 children in a motor home on a journey to Arkansas. We had a breakdown along the way, ended up "stranded" in an RV park, and had to spend an extra 2 days parked about 100 miles from our destination. My children, however, thought it was wonderful! The RV park had an ice cream parlor and a swimming pool only 20 feet away, and I had a new experience that turned into a great vacation.

This vacation adventure and starting my own business were two things that built my confidence during a difficult time, and made lasting memories for my family.

Having a goal is a state of happiness.—E.J. Bartek

Questions to consider:

1) What are my goals?

2) What have I been wishing I could do?

3) What steps can I take to go ahead and do it? (Review tactic 2)

41. Measure your progress

Don't be afraid to set goals for yourself and to measure your progress. Too often vague goals are set, with no real action following. I found myself saying "I can't" all too frequently when thinking of something I'd like to do. I finally realized "why can't I"?

Write down your goals, the steps that you need to take to reach them, and place a timeline on them. By working in conjunction with my four step process listed in tip 2, you can easily move forward on something important to you. I often say that the Nike ad "Just Do It" is wonderful, but I would like to encourage you to "Just Do Something"!

Whatever you choose, it will be a needed distraction and will help you enjoy your days.

There is no happiness except in the realization that we have accomplished something.—Henry Ford

---

Questions to consider:

1) What do I want to accomplish?

2) Using tactics 40 and 2….. what *will* I do?

42. Keep a journal

It amazes me how much we forget about events that occur just one year ago!

Journals are an easy way to unload your feelings at the end of the day, to write down great things that you've done, or to record newsworthy events to review later. The act of writing becomes therapy, while the journal itself becomes history.

My husband enjoyed reading the notes for this book, my journal entries, and to be reminded of the emails we sent to one another. Small details are often lost if not recorded in this manner.

Since our separation and his involvement in Afghanistan were some of the most important events of our marriage, we wanted to ensure that we had this piece of time recorded.

Fear not for the future, weep not for the past. –Percy Bysshe Shelley

---

Questions to consider:

1) Do I enjoy writing?

2) Would I prefer another method of recording the events I experience?

3) What would I most like to remember?

43. Establish email networks

Some of the greatest (and worst) connections can be made in emailing other military spouses. If the group is uplifting, encouraging, and genuinely interested in solving problems and helping one another, then it can be a great way to escape, spend time with others who understand your situation, and get support.

If it becomes a constantly depressing venue, then use your best judgment regarding how much involvement (if any) you need. The primary goal during a deployment is to garner positive, happy relationships!

Take the first step and reach out to other family members from your spouse's unit. You may also find the following websites helpful: www.militarywives.com and www.cinchouse.com. They have various forums for spouses to share emails, purchase online items, or read articles. It is often helpful to remember that you are not alone.

What do we live for if not to make life less difficult for each other?— George Elliot

Questions to consider:

1) Do I want to talk with other military spouses?

2) Do the conversations I have make me feel uplifted and positive?

3) Websites I enjoy:
    a. _____
    b. _____
    c. _____

4) Email addresses of other spouses and families:
    a. _____
    b. _____
    c. _____

44. Take care of business!

While in charge on the home front, ensure that you take care of the necessary business ... without complaining or causing your spouse's job to be more difficult!

On one occasion, my husband called me to ask how the house and car were holding up. I replied "fine". The truth was that we had some car repairs just that week, some other unexpected expenses, and a number of scheduling issues that affected the family and my business. This amounted to a very difficult week!

I saw no value in making him feel bad because he wasn't here to deal with this himself, however, so "fine" was the word I used. He later told me that he and the other men with him were so appreciative of the wives who held it together and took over the responsibility that was needed. He was allowed to focus on the matters at hand, and to be successful in his mission.

My family knows now that when I say "fine" it means:

  F= freaked out
  I= insecure
  N= neurotic
  E= emotional

...but from my husband's perspective at the time, it meant "fine".

The best place to find a helping hand is at the end of your own arm.—
Swedish proverb

Questions to consider:

1) What can I handle on my own?

2) What responsibilities can I relieve from my spouse?

45. Celebrate your successes!

I found that many of the ladies I spoke with saw their small daily triumphs as insignificant, and therefore failed to celebrate, reward themselves, or just feel good about their accomplishments.

After being without your spouse for a period of months, dealing with children who have their own emotional issues surrounding the separation of the family, working all day, taking care of everything to keep the house running, and trying to have a positive attitude through it all…. Something as small as cleaning out the garage should be seen as a success!

Any small step forward toward your overall goals is worthy of a celebration. Don't ignore these steps to the prize of happiness.

Start by doing what is necessary, then what's possible and suddenly you are doing the impossible.—Saint Francis of Assisi

---

Questions to consider:

1) What I have done well?

2) What am I proud of?

3) How will I celebrate?

       a. _____
       b. _____
       c. _____
       d. _____

46. Don't listen to gossip about orders!

This tactic was worthy of repeating again in this section. Just as in the pre-deployment phase, it is important to remember that things change rapidly, conflicting information is the norm, and that nothing you hear should upset you (he's staying longer) or excite you (he's coming home early) until it is official.

Once orders are written, they can still change!

My husband and I had a deal: He wouldn't share any gossip with me, or any information on his homecoming unless it was 80% or more likely. In this way, we avoided useless emotional upheavals and I knew that what I heard from others was less than 80% likely! By knowing this, I could take the gossip in stride, and wait until my husband felt confident in the information before reacting to it.

The one unchangeable certainty is that nothing is certain or unchangeable.—John F. Kennedy

---

Questions to consider:

1) When will I believe "rumors"?

2) How will I react to calls from well-meaning gossips?

Family

47. Stay positive

Again, the words "stay positive" appear in this section. As a mother, I saw so clearly how my children were affected by their "Daddy's" deployment, and how they looked to me to determine how they should interpret comments from others or how they should feel. My children acted anxious and afraid whenever they saw me obsessed with a news segment, or when people would say "Is Brian OK?" When I was strong, centered, and calm… so were they.

We looked at every positive aspect of his deployment, including educating them about the people he was helping, and showing how they needed him right now.

I knew that we were successful when JP, our four year old, was praying one morning. In his prayer, he said "Lord, please send Daddy to Iraq after Afghanistan." When I asked why he prayed that prayer, he said simply "because there are still bad guys in Iraq and the good people there need Daddy to help them".

Although I was so touched and emotional after hearing this from the mouth of my little boy, I knew that he understood. He taught me something very valuable at that moment; as I was not praying this prayer.

Happiness does not depend on outward things, but on the way we see them.
–Leo Tolstoy

Questions to consider:

1) What will keep my children in a positive state of mind?

2) How can I continue to reinforce the positive aspects of this situation?

48. Tell your children the truth

I believe that children of any age can understand on some level what your spouse is being called to do. While avoiding certain words that could cause stress, it was very easy to explain to my 2 and 4 year olds that Daddy was in the military.

We talked about what soldiers are called to do, and why. We discussed that it is the greatest job to aspire to, as they protect our country and our way of life. The kids understood this, and understood that Daddy volunteered for this assignment because of his commitment to his job and our country.

I made sure that they were proud and honored to be serving their country by "giving up" Daddy for a while. They communicated this to others beautifully and made me very proud.

Simple truths are a relief from grand speculations.—Vauvenargues

---

Questions to consider?

1) What will I tell my children?

2) What do I believe about my spouse?

3) How can I share this with the children?

49. Educate your children

I had not owned a globe in many years, but purchased one when the deployment began, so that the children would understand where Daddy was, in relation to other states in our country, to the beach we went to, and other known areas. We used this globe to demonstrate the time difference where Daddy was, and my nephew (also 4) used the phrase: "I wish I was in Afghanistan" every night at bedtime; as he knew that it was morning there!

In addition to the globe, we also used the Internet to research the country of Afghanistan, and learn of its weather, plant life, and animals. Camels became a favorite of my boys, and they had many questions for Daddy when he called. Daddy even sent pictures of herds of camels, that the boys framed and hung up on the wall.

It was a nice, positive way for them to talk about Daddy, have an educational experience, and keep us focused on doing things together.

Education is learning what you didn't even know you didn't know. –Daniel Boorstin

Questions to consider:

1) How can I interest the children in learning about something new?

2) What can we talk about together?

50. Send letters and packages frequently

My husband was in a remote area of Afghanistan for most of his deployment, but was able to periodically get packages from us. The boys and I made an "event" out of shopping for things to send, packaging the box, and taking it to the mail center that we used. It made them feel important to participate, and helped them feel that they were supporting Daddy.

We also included lots of pictures for Daddy. The children had a wonderful time posing for pictures, and yelling at me to "Get the camera, Mommy!" We recorded days at the park, trips to the family ranch, Sea World, and other great places that Daddy was "missing". He enjoyed seeing that the kids were having fun, and we enjoyed including him by posing specifically for him.

In return, my husband took many digital photos during his time in Afghanistan, and mailed us CD's frequently. We received pictures of children in an orphanage that he and some other soldiers were assisting, more camels and donkeys, and many pictures of some of the Afghan people in their villages and stores. The pictures we have from this time period in our lives will always be cherished, and our children were exposed to new cultures and experiences through these pictures.

In the present, every day is a miracle. –James Gould Cozzens

Questions to consider:

1) What will we send in packages?

2) How can the children take part?

3) How can we make it fun for everyone?

51. Record the children's events

In addition to the pictures described in the previous tactic, we bought some very inexpensive micro cassette recorders, and used them to record tapes of daily conversations, special songs, and messages to Daddy. We sent him a recorder with a tape in it, and then only sent the tapes. He loved hearing what the boys were doing, and they felt like they were talking directly to him. These are priceless memories that we now have recorded forever.

I made lists of cute sayings, made video footage of their plays and dancing, and tried to record everything I could. They felt good about preparing something for Daddy to see or hear, and he was happy with getting to see what he missed.

It is the essence of genius to make use of the simplest ideas.—Charles Peguy

Questions to consider:

1) What events can we create?

2) What events are coming up that I need to record?

3) What events do I take for granted that my spouse would be thrilled to see?

52. Take family outings

We traveled more during this deployment than ever before, primarily to keep us all sane and entertained. We went with my in-laws to their farm in Arkansas, to the beach in Corpus Christi, Texas, and to Sea World. We went with my parents to my Aunt's ranch in West Texas, and to many other places around Austin, Texas.

These outings gave the kids much to look forward to, educated them on new experiences, and kept us all fresh and having a good time. None of these were expensive (my in-laws' motor home was our mode of transportation), but all were wonderful experiences.

Though traveling with small children can be challenging, I found that it was easier than keeping the same routine.

Action may not always bring happiness, but there is no happiness without action. –William James

---

Questions to consider:

1) What areas can we explore together?

2) Who can we visit?

3) Where have I been eager to go?

53. Set up time with other military families

This tactic was given to me by friends who have older children. They strongly recommend that families get together to allow the children to talk to each other about how they're feeling, about their family situation, and about things they've done to improve the situation.

Teenagers, in particular, seem to talk about their feelings with one another more than with a parent, and seemed to get great benefit from this interaction! A teenager is much more adept than a preschooler at seeing Mom's emotions, or feeling responsible for the house or chores. This can be overwhelming, and finding that others are experiencing the same emotions can be helpful.

The Texas National Guard and the Family Readiness Units are working to address these issues as well, so that the children have opportunities during meetings to talk with one another and with counselors, and to have their needs acknowledged outside of their own family. Check with your Family Readiness Unit to determine if they are currently providing these services; and if not… volunteer to start the program!

The true way to soften one's troubles is to solace those of others.—Madame De Maintenon

---

Questions to consider:

1) Who are good contacts for my children?

2) How will I facilitate this interaction?

54. Understand your children's emotions

No matter how hard you try to keep things as positive as possible, there are still emotions within your children that need to be recognized. My oldest would have "meltdowns" about an hour after talking to Daddy, or immediately after seeing new pictures of him. My youngest would want Daddy at bedtime, and would cry a little or whine for him. Both acted a little differently at preschool, including more instances of acting out frustrations.

By keeping the preschool staff, the church nursery workers, and family all apprised of our family situation, I had many supporters who helped my children through their feelings when they were away from me.

Always share with those close to you and your children the behaviors you are seeing, and let them help you. Though these emotions are painful for a mother to see, they are an important part of the child's "venting" process. Just as I cried, it was important to let my boys cry, too. We spent a few evenings huddled together praying, with a few tears and a lot of hugs.

It takes courage to lead a life. Any life. –Erica Jong

Questions to consider:

1) What are my children feeling?

2) What new behaviors am I seeing in them?

3) What can I do to help alleviate their fears, stress, or worry?

55. Keep discipline consistent

Even though the children are experiencing new emotions and some adjustments, it is still critical to keep the same discipline plan and the same limits. Although I understood *why* my children might exhibit an undesirable behavior, the behavior was still inappropriate. We had very few situations that were not easily cleared up, by staying consistent, telling them I understood that they missed Daddy, but continuing to enforce the expected behaviors. Internally I was very upset that they were affected, but knew that it would be easier for them if the family expectations remained the same.

"Wait until your father gets home" and "Why are you treating me this way" are probably discipline techniques that are not going to work for you over the term of a deployment. Not only do they make the spouse who is away the "bad guy", but they decrease your own effectiveness and the respect your children have for you as the primary disciplinarian.

I noticed that I was very emotional in the 2nd month after my husband arrived in Afghanistan, and that the children seemed to be behaving terribly. After analyzing the situation, they were also affected emotionally, of course, but they also felt insecure with my emotional state! Once I realized this and began to discipline them more decisively and unemotionally, they immediately began listening and behaving properly.

He is happiest, be he king or peasant, who finds peace in his home.
–Johann von Goethe

Questions to consider:

1) What are our family's discipline policies and expectations?

2) Have I historically been the primary disciplinarian?

3) What actions will I take to lovingly establish myself in this role?

56. Work on projects together

As frustrating as it can be for the parent at home, enlisting your children's help with projects around the house makes for an interesting activity, and a great bonding opportunity.

The children feel important, share with your spouse that they're "working" and "helping", and things get done as a family.

We planted a garden together, set up an inflatable (very large) pool together, and even painted the occasional items. It took me much longer and certainly created more laundry, but the outcome was positive for all of us.

Look at your surroundings to see if there is a project waiting to happen. Get the children involved, and have fun!

Enjoy the little things, for one day you may look back and realize that they were the big things.—Robert Brault

---

Questions to consider:

1) What are projects that need to be done?

2) How can the children help me?

3) Shopping list for projects:

    a. _____
    b. _____
    c. _____

57. Establish a routine

I and many of the other parents I spoke with agree that an established routine is easier for everyone involved. We would get up at the same time each day (week days), get dressed and do breakfast in the same order, and complete any other tasks similarly every day. Likewise, the after school, dinner, bath and bedtime routine stayed relatively the same.

This eliminated needless arguments and discussions, and helped establish the flow of events for all parties! When dealing with small children, being proactive in eliminating possible arguments goes a long way!

Family life is the source of the greatest human happiness. –Robert J. Havighurst

Questions to consider:

1) What activities need to be accomplished?

2) How will I do this alone?

3) What schedule works best for our family?

58. Shake up the routine

Now that you have a routine, a great way to enter in some spontaneous fun is to totally shake it up once in a while.

Some mornings the kids would go downstairs expecting breakfast to be on the table, but we'd load up in the car and get donuts instead. Some afternoons we'd stop after school at the park, or go to my parents' house instead beginning our usual dinner routine.

These fairly insignificant events were very exciting for young children, because it was a break from the normal routine. The routine then is easy to implement again afterwards, (until you sense the need to shake it up.)

When patterns are broken, new worlds emerge. –Tuli Kupferberg

Questions to consider:

1) What are some surprise activities I can throw into our routine?

2) What would the children enjoy?

59. Make the most of long-distance communication

Each situation varies with the deployed spouse regarding their ability to communicate with their family. Some have daily email access and can call frequently. Some can only call occasionally. We were fortunate enough to have been given our own satellite phone, which allowed my husband to call us almost once per week.

I would like to encourage you to use this time to talk about uplifting, positive accomplishments, and to give encouragement to one another. I also found it to be very positive for us to have the children talk on the phone to Daddy.

These calls or emails can become a very sad, depressing time if not handled properly, whereas they can be a great source of joy if everyone takes part and shares positively with one another. I tried to keep in mind the question: "Can my husband do anything about this particular issue?" If the answer was "no", then I didn't bring it up. I felt that he had enough pressure, homesickness, and stress in carrying out his own job and duty. Part of my job and duty was to handle what I could, and to do it positively.

Do not look back on happiness, or dream of it in the future. You are only sure of today; do not let yourself be cheated out of it. –Henry Ward Beecher

Questions to consider:

1) What do we want to tell Daddy (or Mommy)?

2) Lists to remember:

60. Keep kids away from CNN

Though it is an amazing technological advancement to have play by play news coverage of a war, it is quite difficult on those of us close to the troops in harms way. I know how I felt watching the news, and as an adult understood it all. I could only imagine what the images and commentary would do to a child who had limited understanding of the concepts being discussed.

The words "kill", "dead", and "bomb" certainly are understood by the children. Our troops, and those of other countries, tend to be dressed alike and look similar on TV. A child's active imagination could cause nightmares, fears and anxiety simply by seeing some of these images.

I urge you to keep the children away from these images, and explain to them what you believe they are capable of understanding.

Children have neither a past nor a future. Thus they enjoy the present, which seldom happens to us. –Jean de La Bruyere

Questions to consider:

1) What should my children know?

2) How I can I best explain these concepts in an age-appropriate manner?

61. Explain others' behaviors

There were several occasions when other adults would approach me in front of my children to ask me if I saw that "such and such a unit was ambushed" or when they would exhibit extreme sadness or sympathy for us.

My 4 year old made me aware of this, when he let me know how worried he was about someone who had cried and said she was praying for my husband. He didn't understand that her sympathy was very nice, and that her prayers were needed. He just saw a woman crying about his Daddy and was afraid for her and us alike.

I recommend that you explain the behavior of others immediately in a way the kids can understand. I found that the things I chose to ignore tended to be things that worried my children afterward. By immediately commenting, I soothed their tension and let them understand what people were feeling.

The true test of character is...how we behave when we don't know what to do. –John Holt

---

Questions to consider:

1) What occasions may have influenced the children?

2) How should I respond to people in the future?

62. Count your blessings together

Our family prayer time was (and still is) so special. During this time, the boys and I would thank God for everything that we have been blessed with, including a Daddy who sacrifices for others. We thanked God for our health, home, food, clothing, toys, family, US troops, church and many other items kids think of (candy, gum, etc.).

This helped the children see how blessed we really are, and how we should be proud that we sent Daddy to help others who need him.

They loved this poem that was sent to me via email:

Thank God for dirty dishes; they have a tale to tell.
While other folks go hungry, we're eating pretty well.
With home and health and happiness, we shouldn't want to fuss;
For by this stack of evidence, God's very good to us. —Anon

Questions to consider:

1) For what am I thankful?

2) How can my children learn to express their thanks?

Encouragement for America's Hidden Heroes

Your relationship

63. Stay positive

I am certain that I have said the words "I love you" to my husband every day we've had together. During his deployment, there were many days when we didn't have this opportunity. I ensured that our calls and written communications were filled with "I love you", "I'm proud of you" and "I'm honored to be your wife".

These positive statements, along with listening to his needs and being someone he could confide in helped to strengthen our relationship and bond during this difficult time.

It's very easy to feel down or sorry for yourself during this time. I found that the quality of my thoughts determined my mood for the day. I kept reminding myself that our soldiers are amazing people, and that there are few jobs to be honored in the same way. This gave me comfort, and allowed me to communicate to him what I truly felt: pride in being his wife.

When one door of happiness closes, another opens; but often we look so long at the closed door that we do not see the one which has been opened for us. –Helen Keller

---

Questions to consider:

1) What positive affirmations can I communicate to my spouse?

2) What do I need to remind myself of?

64. You are serving your country, too!

I've said in other tactics that we, as military spouses, are also serving our country. When you remind yourself of this fact, the hardships and difficulties become much easier to handle and understand than if you feel like the one who was left behind.

By approaching your spouse in this manner, you are forming a team relationship, and the deployment is handled as a team instead of two individuals. This helped us to work toward a common goal, and to understand one another even better than before.

By supporting my family and handling the home-front, I was doing my part. It felt good to know that this was impacting my husband and children, and ultimately the world.

Don't sell yourself and your role short. Lean on each other and work together.

Life becomes harder when we live for others, but it also becomes richer and happier.—Albert Schweitzer

---

Questions to consider:

1) What is my role?

2) How can I best help to serve my country?

65. Make the most of long-distance communication

As mentioned in the section on Family, ensure that calls and emails are positive, informative, or that needed questions and issues are discussed. I recommend making notes regarding things you really need to discuss, so that you're ready with the needed questions when you spouse is able to call.

This way, the needed family business can be taken care of, and the rest of the time may be spent strengthening your bond with one another.

We would often talk about funny things the kids did, what we saw on our trips, and how much we missed one another. I was dedicated to telling him on each call how much he was loved and missed, and how things were going well at home. Our calls were very enjoyable, and were a source of strength for both of us.

Happiness consists of living each day as if it were the first day of your honeymoon and the last day of your vacation. – Anon.

Questions to consider:

1) What questions do I need to ask my spouse?

2) What stories do I want to share?

66. Eliminate guilt from your spouse

Based on information I collected from my husband and other spouses in Afghanistan and Iraq, they often have a feeling of guilt for leaving the family.

Most will know that their service to our country is of paramount importance, and would not have it any other way. The guilt, however, still creeps in because they know that things are difficult for the spouse left at home. They worry that we don't understand, or that we will leave them for something or someone easier to deal with.

The greatest thing that we can do is reassure them that we're OK, we love them, and that we're waiting for them. By giving them this encouragement we are helping them do their jobs, and helping them get home more quickly!

The only gift is a portion of thyself. – Ralph Waldo Emerson

Questions to consider:

1) Is my spouse feeling guilty?

2) Am I making him/her feeling this way?

3) How can I help eliminate this negative emotion?

Encouragement for America's Hidden Heroes

Homecoming

67. Stay positive

It may appear a bit strange to include this tactic in the Homecoming section, but it definitely has a place here. Upon a homecoming, there are many stressful situations that will arise that you may not have experienced before.

I was alone for 9 months, during which time I became quite successful at managing the money for myself and the kids, scheduling all of our time, and handling every situation. Upon his return, there were some immediate potential conflicts that arose: he was spending money without asking me (how dare he!), he wanted input in our schedule, and he would jump into a discipline or family issue. My initial reaction was not positive! I also found that I had difficulty slowing down, relaxing, or making time to just get to know each other again.

However, once I took the time to realize that these inconveniences were all due to the fact that he was finally home, I began to lighten up and see them as positive stressors to have.

Remember that your spouse is home safely. Everything else is insignificant!

For everything you have missed, you have gained something else. –Ralph Waldo Emerson

---

Questions to consider:

1) How might I handle things when my spouse comes home?

2) How can I best enjoy my spouse and our time together?

3) What were the most positive aspects of our separation that I can share with him/her?

68. Research and prepare emotionally

I feel that it is very important to research online, read books, or talk with others who have had a spouse deployed in a combat situation. To expect the same person to return, to pick up the duties and chores where they left off, and to jump right back into life as before is setting yourself and your spouse up for failure.

The changes you see will vary depending on the job your spouse had, what he saw, what he did, and how he felt about their departure from the country he served in.

Many times our spouses will be unsure of how to act, appear disorganized, and need your patience to get them through this readjustment. If you are prepared for the fact that your spouse will need time to adjust, you will make it through this phase much stronger than before. Be patient, talk openly, and work together to bring back a level of normalcy to your home.

Talk with your Family Readiness Unit about having a seminar on the "homecoming". If they are not prepared for this, have them recommend people who have gone through this phase before; as they may be able to help you prepare.

Adversity not only draws people together, but brings forth that beautiful inward friendship. –Soren Kierkegaard

---

Questions to consider:

1) How is my spouse feeling?

2) What have other families experienced that I could learn from?

3) What should I expect?

69. Research and understand medications

I was not aware that some of our troops may be given various medications, such as anti-malarial drugs that can cause side effects that may affect you and your family.

My husband had nightmares, difficulty sleeping, and some anxiety as a result of one such medication. He was jumpy, nervous, and tended to get angry very easily. This can be very frightening behavior if you aren't prepared for it, for both the soldier and the family. In our case it was minor, because we took the time to discuss and research it, and we all knew what to expect. Without this knowledge, it could have become a difficult situation for all of us.

Understand that your spouse is having adjustments in many ways, and that the medications can temporarily influence their behavior. If the reactions are severe, it is very important for you to report it immediately to your spouse's chain of command, or take your spouse to a medical facility, if needed.

We found that ours were managed easily by patience and love at home.

A danger foreseen is half avoided. –Thomas Fuller

Questions to consider:

1) What medications (if any) has my spouse been given?

2) What expectations should I have? (online research helps!)

70. Have realistic expectations for readjustment

In talking with friends who have had their spouses deployed multiple times in the last 2 years, they agree that any deployment has additional "time" added to the end (after your spouse is home) where you are still primarily in charge of the home and family. Because of reasons mentioned above, expecting your spouse to immediately take over and give you a break may cause both of you failure and heartache. Keep in mind that your spouse has not been on vacation either!

Friends of mine who have done Christian missions in various parts of the world demonstrated a feeling of "overwhelm" when returning to the US, and all of our amenities. This is a normal feeling that our troops often experience as well, which will subside with time.

The readjustment into a society where there is such wealth, infinite choices, and a fast paced environment is shocking when the soldier has been living in much different circumstances. Keep this in mind, and allow for a slow adjustment.

The firmest friendships have been formed in mutual adversity, as iron is most strongly united by the fiercest flame. –Charles Caleb Colton

---

Questions to consider:

1) What have others experienced?

2) What expectations do I have that may need to be altered or delayed?

71. Exercise patience with your spouse

Patience is critical in the months following a deployment. I know that part of me wondered if I was doing the right thing by treating my husband so carefully, and allowing a slow transition back into our life and family. That part was wrong to question… as the patience paid off in terms of very few arguments, lots of bonding and another success as a team.

Remember, although you may be ready to head to the spa, to relieve some of your responsibilities, or to run away temporarily, your situation is definitely less stressful than before; as your spouse is safe at home.

By giving a bit more of yourself now, you will find great reward as a couple in just a few short weeks.

This time, like all times, is a very good one if we but know what to do with it. –Ralph Waldo Emerson

---

Questions to consider:

1) How can I remember to be patient?

2) What can I continue to do to eliminate my own stress?

72. Celebrate!

By far the most important tactic is to celebrate your spouse's safe return!

The relief you will feel is unbelievable, but the true comfort may take some time to really permeate you. You've been through quite an ordeal, as has your spouse, and you both need to relax. I found that relaxing took some practice, as it was a new experience again for both of us. Practice together, and celebrate!

Though the combat deployment was the most difficult thing we've encountered thus far in our lives, it has been integral to our development as a strong family. If my husband should return again to combat, we are much more prepared and emotionally conditioned to handle it, and to again succeed gracefully.

We now have new friends, both from Afghanistan and in the US, and the experience *forever changed us* for the better. We understand the world in a way we never did before, and found strength as a family that will always be with us.

May you live all the days of your life. –Jonathan Swift

Questions to consider:

How will we celebrate?

The tactics mentioned in previous chapters helped me to personally navigate what was, at times, a very stressful, difficult, scary, and overwhelming situation. With the help of friends and family, I was able to transform this temporary situation into one of personal growth, relationship building, and strength; and I wish the same for you.

My prayers are with all military families and service members, but particularly those who did not have an opportunity for the homecoming. May God ease your sorrow, and may pride replace it.

The Prayer of the Military Wife

Dear Lord, give me greatness of heart to see the difference between duty and his love for me.

Give me understanding that I may know when duty calls him, he must go.

Give me a task to do each day to fill time when he is away.

And Lord, when he is in a foreign land, keep him safe in your loving hands.

And Lord, when his duty is in the field, please protect him and be his shield.

And Lord, when deployment is so long, please stay with me and keep me strong.

Amen

Resources for the Military family:

Air Force Crossroads: www.afcrossroads.com

Air Force Reserve: www.afreserve.com

Air National Guard: www.ang.af.mil

Army National Guard: www.arng.army.mil

Army Reserve: www.army.mil/usar

Coast Guard Reserve: www.uscg.mil/hq/reserve/reshmpg.html

Department of Defense: www.defenselink.mil

Employer Support of the Guard and Reserve: www.esgr.org

LIFElines: www.lifelines2000.org

Marine Reserves: www.mfr.usmc.mil

MAPsite (Military Assistance Program): http://mfrc.calib.com

MFRC (Military Family Resource Center): http://mfrc.calib.com

National Guard; www.ngb.dtic.mil

Naval Reserve: www.navres.navy.mil/navresfor

Operation Ready: http://trol.redstone.army.mil/acs/virtual2/depmob_orn.html

Reserve Affairs: (Office of Assistant Secretary of Defense): www.defenselink.mil/ra/

TRICARE: www.tricare.osd.mil

United Concordia: www.ucci.com

Virtual Army Community Service Link: http://trol.redstone.army.mil/acs/virtual2

Military wives forums: www.cinchouse.com
www.miliarywives.com

Financial planning assistance: www.savvy.onweb.com

Growing your small business venture: www.gobeyondmarketing.com

About the Author

Amy Stevens is a proud military wife, dynamic businesswoman, mother, speaker, and author. During her husband's recent deployment and service in Afghanistan, she realized the fears, pains, responsibilities and difficulties that arise for families facing War, many for the first time in their lives- and became determined to make the path easier for those following her in this service. Patriotic and proud of her family, she inspires and motivates military spouses to plan, to enjoy, and to move forward with their lives: while embracing the fact that they, too, are heroes.